SQUIRTS AND SPURTS
SCIENCE FUN WITH WATER

VICKI COBB
ILLUSTRATED BY STEVE HAEFELE

THE MILLBROOK PRESS
BROOKFIELD, CONNECTICUT

For Abigail Jane Cobb
—Vicki Cobb

For my lovely wife, Sharon
—S. H.

Published by The Millbrook Press, Inc.
2 Old New Milford Road
Brookfield, CT 06804
www.millbrookpress.com

Library of Congress Cataloging-in-Publication Data
Cobb, Vicki.
Squirts and spurts : science fun with water / Vicki Cobb ; illustrated by Steve Haefele.
p. cm.
Summary: Explains the physics of water pressure, showing how it makes everyday products such as faucets,
spray bottles, and water pistols work. Includes experiments.
ISBN 0-7613-1572-1 (lib. bdg.)
1. Hydrodynamics—Juvenile literature. [1. Water—Experiments. 2. Experiments.] I. Haefele, Steve, ill. II. Title.
QC151.2 .C63 2000
507.8—dc21 00-022113

SQUIRT IT AND SPURT IT

How many ways can you make water squirt out of your mouth? Don't just think about it. Experiment and find out.

Do this experiment at the sink or when you take a bath. Fill your mouth with water and see how many ways you can force the water out.

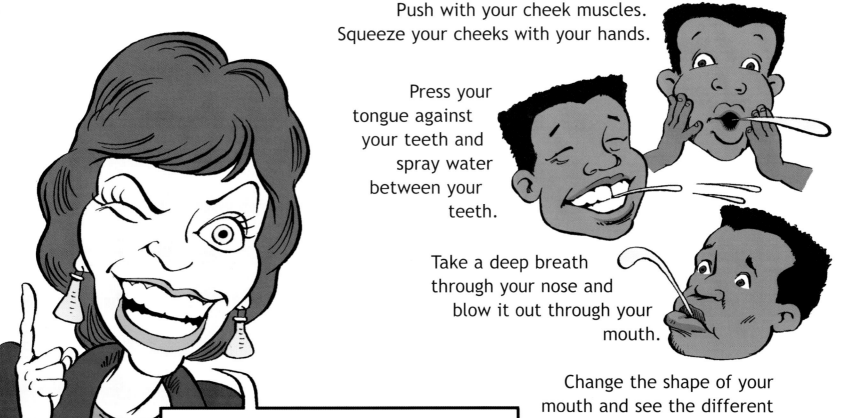

Push with your cheek muscles. Squeeze your cheeks with your hands.

Press your tongue against your teeth and spray water between your teeth.

Take a deep breath through your nose and blow it out through your mouth.

JUST BE CAREFUL WHERE YOU AIM!

Change the shape of your mouth and see the different kinds of streams you can make.

3

You need two things to make a spout of water—a small opening for the water to pass through and some way to push the water through the opening. You can make one small opening with your lips or use the little openings between your teeth. When you squirt water out of your mouth, you use your cheek muscles, your hands, your tongue, and air in your lungs to push on the water. Whenever you use your muscles to move something, you are creating a force.

Can you use more than one force at a time?

WHAT HAPPENS IF YOU BLOW WITH YOUR LUNGS WHILE YOU SQUEEZE YOUR CHEEKS WITH YOUR HANDS? THAT'S USING TWO FORCES AT THE SAME TIME. IT'S THE ULTIMATE MOUTH SQUIRT!

How about having a water-squirting contest with a friend? Do it outside, if you want to stay out of trouble, and don't squirt anything except water.

There are many inventions that shoot water and other liquids. Some make spouts and some make sprays and some make both. Inventions that squirt and spray liquids make our lives easier. Go on an invention hunt around your house. How many can you find? What problems do they solve? Here are some examples to get you started:

Once you understand how these inventions work you can make some squirting and spraying devices of your own.

I CALL THE PEOPLE WHO DESIGNED THESE THINGS "SQUIRT ENGINEERS." YOU CAN BE ONE, TOO.

6

2 GRAVITY SPRAY BOTTLE

When you tilt the opening of a can of soda toward the ground, the liquid pours out. You don't need to waste a can of soda to discover this. The soda pours because a force called gravity pulls it toward the center of the earth. Gravity also pulls you. How hard it pulls depends on how big you are. Gravity's pull on you is your weight.

Water also has weight. The weight of water pressing on surfaces is known as water pressure. The next experiment uses gravity to produce pressure that sprays water. It also shows you what happens to a stream of water when you increase the pressure.

HERE IS WHAT YOU NEED:

an empty plastic soda bottle, the larger the better

masking tape

I THINK I HURT MYSELF!

a pushpin, thumbtack, or safety pin

magnifying glass

8

Use the pin or tack to make four holes in the bottle. One hole should be near the bottom of the bottle, one near the top, and two in the middle. They should be evenly spaced, about 2 inches (5 centimeters) apart. Cover the holes with pieces of masking tape. Now fill the bottle with water. Put the bottle in the tub or sink or take it outside. Pull off the tape.

Which hole has the strongest squirt? How can you tell? Which has the weakest? Where in the bottle is the weight of the water the greatest? Is it near the hole that shows the strongest force of water?

Take a close look at one of the spurts. Use a magnifying glass if you wish. See where the water breaks up into drops. Is it about the same place for all the sprays?

THE DROPS FORM BECAUSE OF A FORCE CALLED SURFACE TENSION THAT SEPARATES THE WATER INTO TINY BALLS. SURFACE TENSION ACTS LIKE A "SKIN" THAT HOLDS A DROP OF WATER TOGETHER. AT THE BEGINNING OF EACH SPURT, THERE IS AN UNBROKEN STREAM OF WATER. BUT THERE COMES A POINT WHERE SURFACE TENSION IS STRONG ENOUGH TO SEPARATE THE STREAM INTO A STRING OF TINY DROPS.

As long as you have the pin, why not make a few more holes? What happens to the spurts when you make bigger holes in the bottle than the pin can make? Use a nail and find out.

10

A SUPER-LEAKY SPRAY BAG

Water presses on all the surfaces it touches. It presses on the bottom of a bottle and on its sides. The bottle with holes in the last experiment showed that water pressure is greatest at the bottom of the bottle. But it also showed that there is pressure near the top. When you squeeze a container of water, you add your force to the water pressure.

A SQUEEZE BOTTLE GIVES ME CONTROL OVER MY KETCHUP. I GET EXACTLY AS MUCH AS I SQUEEZE OUT.

You use many soft-sided bottles for squirting everything from ketchup to shampoo. When you squeeze this kind of bottle, the liquid comes out the only place it can—where the hole is.

Now suppose there are several holes in a squeezable container. What do you think will happen when you add pressure by squeezing? Which squirts are really going to spurt? Experiment and find out. This is another experiment for the bathtub.

HERE IS WHAT YOU NEED:

a pushpin, thumbtack, or safety pin

a sandwich-size plastic bag

Make about twenty double holes in the bag by sticking the pin through both sides at once.

Fill the bag with water and twist it closed. Hold it by the top with one hand and squeeze it with the other. Water squirts through all the holes.

SHOWERS

No surprise. Look at the direction and size of the squirts. Does gravity affect the squirts? Pinch a corner of the bag, squeeze it in the middle, poke it on the top. Watch as every squirt responds the same to your force. No matter where you press, your force is spread evenly throughout the water. Amazing! The added pressure of your fingers has the same effect on every hole.

Force that travels through a liquid is called hydraulic pressure. "Hydra" comes from a Greek word that means water. "Aulic" means tube or pipe. Hydraulic pressure can do some pretty fantastic things.

Suppose you want to lift something very heavy, like a car. Well, the lifts in service stations use hydraulic pressure to lift great loads.

These large jacks use oil instead of water as the liquid because it doesn't evaporate and it won't rust the metal around it.

Air is pumped into a round container of oil, called the master cylinder.

PRESSURIZED AIR

MASTER CYLINDER

OIL

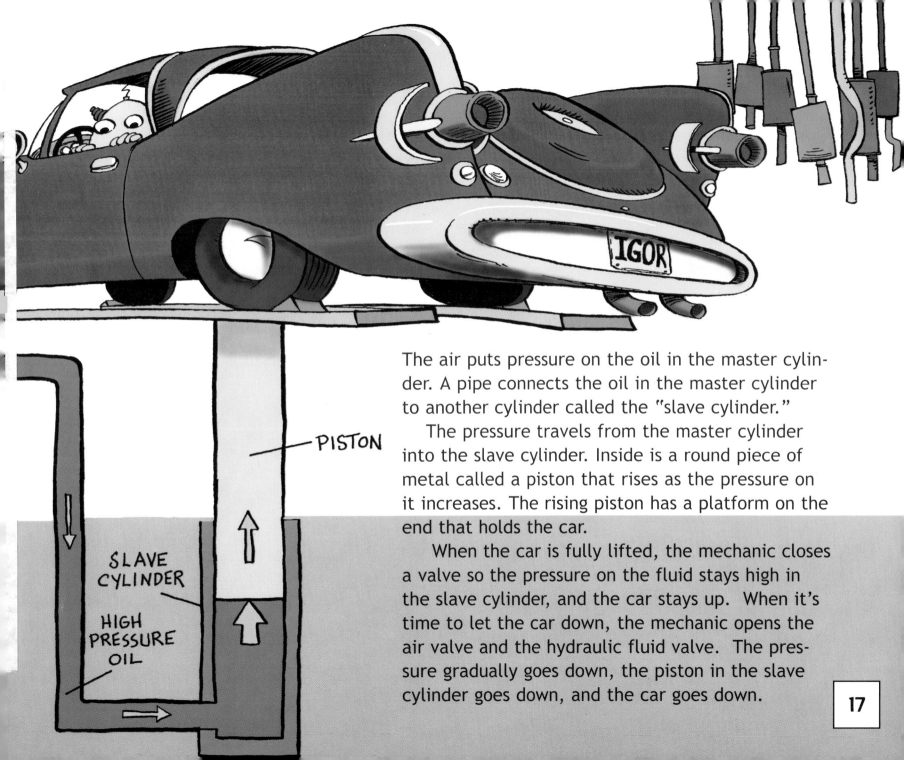

PISTON

SLAVE CYLINDER

HIGH PRESSURE OIL

The air puts pressure on the oil in the master cylinder. A pipe connects the oil in the master cylinder to another cylinder called the "slave cylinder."

The pressure travels from the master cylinder into the slave cylinder. Inside is a round piece of metal called a piston that rises as the pressure on it increases. The rising piston has a platform on the end that holds the car.

When the car is fully lifted, the mechanic closes a valve so the pressure on the fluid stays high in the slave cylinder, and the car stays up. When it's time to let the car down, the mechanic opens the air valve and the hydraulic fluid valve. The pressure gradually goes down, the piston in the slave cylinder goes down, and the car goes down.

A VALVE IS LIKE A DOOR FOR LIQUIDS. A FAUCET HAS A VALVE THAT STOPS WATER WHEN IT IS CLOSED. THE WATER IS UNDER PRESSURE. WHEN YOU OPEN THE VALVE, WATER FLOWS. THE TOPS OF CERTAIN SQUEEZE BOTTLES ARE VALVES. PULL TO OPEN, PRESS DOWN TO CLOSE. WHEN YOU PRESS A SQUEEZE BOTTLE, YOU CREATE HYDRAULIC PRESSURE ON THE LIQUID INSIDE. THE LIQUID RESPONDS TO THE PRESSURE BY MOVING THE ONLY PLACE IT CAN GO, OUT THE VALVE.

MOVABLE CAP

FIXED PLUG

SQUEEZE BOTTLE

LIQUID

Hydraulic pressure can change a small force into a large one. Most cars have hydraulic brakes. The small pressure of a foot on a brake pedal is changed into a larger force that can slow down a moving car.

A BARREL AND PLUNGER SQUIRTER

Normal air pressure comes from the weight of the air all around us. All the air around the earth is called the atmosphere. It may not seem that air has weight, but it presses with a force of 15 pounds on every square inch (6.75 kilograms on every 6 square centimeters).

NORMALLY, YOU CAN'T FEEL AIR PRESSURE BECAUSE THE PRESSURE INSIDE YOUR BODY IS THE SAME AS THE PRESSURE OUTSIDE. JUST AS WATER PRESSURE IS GREATEST AT THE BOTTOM OF A BODY OF WATER, AIR PRESSURE IS GREATEST AT THE BOTTOM OF THE ATMOSPHERE—AT SEA LEVEL. HAVE YOU NOTICED THAT YOUR EARS SOMETIMES 'POP' WHEN YOU GO UP IN AN ELEVATOR? THAT'S BECAUSE AIR PRESSURE DROPS WHEN YOU RISE. THE OUTSIDE PRESSURE ON YOUR EARDRUMS IS LESS THAN YOUR INSIDE PRESSURE AND YOU FEEL IT!

Air pressure pushes on everything, including the liquid in a glass. When you use a straw, you move water by sucking. Your mouth is a pump that takes air out of the straw. This lowers the air pressure on the liquid in the straw. The pressure of the atmosphere on your drink is now greater than the pressure inside the straw. The weight of the atmosphere pushes the liquid up the straw.

22

Any time you remove some of the air from a space and lower the air pressure, you create something called a partial vacuum. A partial vacuum can act like a pump. A pump is a machine that makes a liquid or a gas move against a force such as gravity.

A VACUUM CLEANER MAKES A PARTIAL VACUUM INSIDE THE MACHINE. OUTSIDE AIR RUSHES IN AND BRINGS DIRT WITH IT.

In this next experiment you create a partial vacuum with a barrel and plunger, also known as a cylinder and piston.

(Remember the hydraulic lift? It also uses a cylinder and piston.)

The barrel is a tube that is closed at one end, except for a small opening. The plunger is a cylinder that exactly fits inside the barrel from the open end so that it is fairly airtight.

HERE IS WHAT YOU NEED:

The barrel is an empty container of Crystal Light® lemonade. It measures 6$\frac{1}{2}$ inches high. Tear off the label. Hammer a nail through the center of the bottom to make a hole.

The plunger is a small unopened bottle (11.2 oz) of Evian Natural Spring Water®.

WRONG NAIL!

2. Put the frozen plunger into your barrel so that the bottom of the plunger is resting on the bottom of the barrel.

Now lower them both into a basin of water. Slowly pull the plunger out of the barrel. Water flows in through the hole to fill the partial vacuum you make when you pull back the plunger.

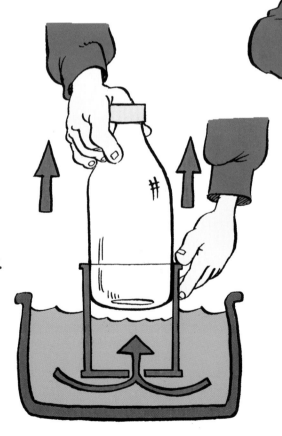

1. If you insert the plunger into the barrel you will notice it is a bit loose. The way to tighten things up is to put the bottle into the freezer. The water will expand when it freezes and give you the tight fit you want.

3. When the end of the plunger is about four inches from the bottom of the barrel, remove them both from the water. When you push the plunger back into the container, the water is forced out the hole.

THE POWER OF THE SPURT DEPENDS ON HOW FAST YOU PUSH YOUR PLUNGER.

Your doctor uses a barrel and plunger called a syringe to give you shots. A hollow needle is attached to the barrel of a syringe. The bottle of medicine is held upside down. The needle is stuck into the bottle with the plunger completely filling the barrel. As the plunger is drawn back a partial vacuum is created. The medicine flows through the needle into the barrel of the syringe.

When you get a shot, the plunger is pushed quickly back into the barrel, shooting the liquid into your body.

I'M SHRINKING!

HERE'S HOW IT WORKS.

A water pistol is a squirt engineer's dream. It's a kind of barrel and plunger that's known as a piston pump. Like most pumps, a water pistol has valves. Shake an empty water pistol and hear the valves rattle.

Squeeze the trigger and the piston goes in. Air is forced out of the chamber and the intake valve closes. The first squeeze squirts air, not water.

Release the trigger and the spring forces back the piston. Air pressure is now lower in the chamber. Air pressure outside the chamber forces the intake valve to open and liquid moves in.

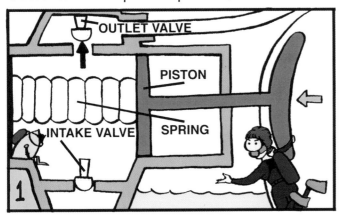

OUTLET VALVE

PISTON

INTAKE VALVE

SPRING

1

2

Squeeze the trigger and the piston pushes the liquid out of the chamber.

Release the trigger and more liquid flows in.

3

4

THE SPRAY PUMPS FOR CERTAIN HOUSE-
HOLD CLEANERS WORK THE SAME WAY AS A
WATER PISTOL. YOU CAN FEEL THE PARTIAL
VACUUM THEY CREATE. UNSCREW THE TOP
OF A SPRAY BOTTLE, REMOVE IT,
AND RINSE OFF THE BOTTOM OF
THE TUBE. REST THE END OF
THE TUBE ON A FINGER OF
ONE HAND WHILE YOU

PUMP WITH THE OTHER. AFTER A FEW
PUMPS TO CREATE A PARTIAL VACUUM,
PULL THE TUBE AWAY FROM YOUR FINGER.
FEEL THE SUCTION? THE PRESSURE OF
THE ATMOSPHERE OUTSIDE THE TUBE
PUSHES THE SKIN ON YOUR FINGER INTO
THE TUBE IN THE SAME WAY THAT CLEAN-
ING LIQUID IS FORCED UP INTO THE
SPRAYER NOZZLE.

A BALLOON WATER SHOOTER

Rubber is a material that is said to have a "memory." You can stretch a balloon and change its shape. If you release it, the balloon snaps back to its original shape. You stretch a balloon when you blow it up. When you let go of the open end, the balloon shrinks, forcing out the air.

This same force can be used to shoot a jet of water. The next experiment can get things pretty wet, so check with an adult before you start.

31

A BALLOON'S MEMORY CREATES A FORCE AS IT SPRINGS BACK INTO SHAPE.

You will need a 12-inch (30-centimeter) round balloon. Make sure it comes from a package that says "12 inches" and "helium quality." These balloons are made of stronger rubber than balloons you blow up by mouth. Stretch the end over a faucet and fill the balloon with water until it is about eight inches (20 centimeters) around. Turn off the water and pull the balloon off the faucet. Pinch the top closed until you are in a safe place to let go. As the balloon "remembers" its original shape, the water is forced out in a powerful jet.

AH, YES-
SWEET REVENGE!

NO FAIR! THIS IS
THE BIGGEST
WATER SQUIRTER
IN THE BOOK!

SWOOSH!

Turkey basters and eye droppers also use the amazing ability of rubber to "remember" its original shape. Both of these inventions have a rubber bulb at the end of a tube. When you squeeze a turkey baster or an eye dropper, you make the inside space smaller. When you let go, it springs back to its original shape.

First you squeeze the bulb, forcing out air. Then you put the tip of the tube in a liquid. When you let go of the bulb, it springs back into its original larger shape. Now there is less air in the bulb and you have made a partial vacuum. The air pressure inside the tube and bulb is now lower than the air pressure outside. The outside air pushes liquid into the tube.

 # A SODA STRAW SPRAYER

Another way to create a partial vacuum is to use the force of moving air. When air moves rapidly across the top of an open tube, it creates a partial vacuum and the pressure in the tube drops. This vacuum can be used to pump a liquid up a tube. Atomizers on perfume bottles and spray pumps for certain house-cleaning products work this way. If the end of the tube is in a liquid, the pressure of the atmosphere pushes the liquid up the tube. When the liquid gets to the top, the moving air turns it into a spray.

EAU de IGOR

See for yourself.

HERE IS WHAT YOU NEED:

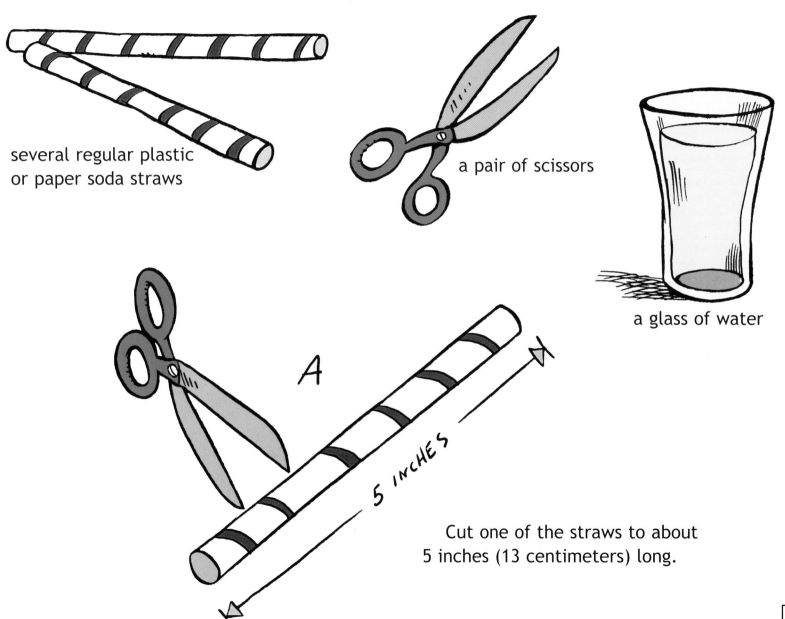

several regular plastic
or paper soda straws

a pair of scissors

a glass of water

A

5 INCHES

Cut one of the straws to about
5 inches (13 centimeters) long.

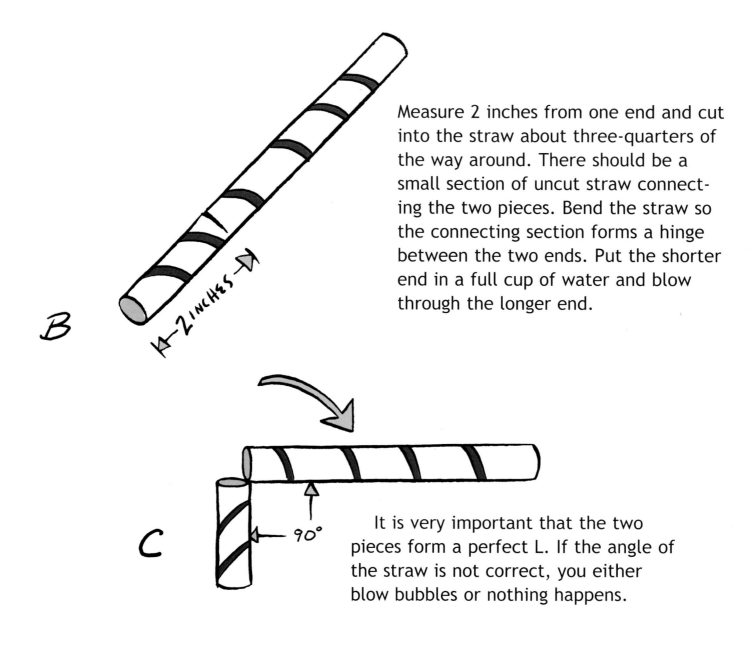

Measure 2 inches from one end and cut into the straw about three-quarters of the way around. There should be a small section of uncut straw connecting the two pieces. Bend the straw so the connecting section forms a hinge between the two ends. Put the shorter end in a full cup of water and blow through the longer end.

B

←2 INCHES→

C

90°

It is very important that the two pieces form a perfect L. If the angle of the straw is not correct, you either blow bubbles or nothing happens.

You may need to use several straws until you get this to work. Some straws work better than others.

HERE ARE SOME TIPS:

1. Fill a glass close to the top so that the water doesn't have far to rise. If your spray gun is working, you can see the water level rise in the straw as you blow across the top.

2. It may help to flatten the end of the straw you're blowing through near the hinge.

3. Patience helps. If at first you don't succeed, keep on trying. Most scientific discoveries come after years of experiments. But this one shouldn't take that long.

A BUBBLING FOAM BOMB

When you push the button on the nozzle of a can of whipped cream or shaving cream, out comes foam. Look at some foam with a magnifying lens. Foam is just lots of bubbles stuck together.

The cans that make foam are called aerosol cans.

SPRING

LIQUID PROPELLANT

LIQUID PRODUCT

TUBE

AN AEROSOL SPRAY CAN CONTAINS A SPECIAL LIQUID CHEMICAL UNDER PRESSURE. IT CHANGES TO A GAS AT ROOM TEMPERATURE. THE CHEMICAL IS CALLED A PROPELLANT. THE PROPELLANT IS PUT IN THE CAN UNDER HIGH PRESSURE THAT MAKES IT A LIQUID WHILE IT IS IN THE CAN.

ALSO IN THE CAN IS THE LIQUID PRODUCT—WHIPPING CREAM, HAIR SPRAY, PAINT, OR SOMETHING ELSE.

WHEN YOU PUSH DOWN ON THE
NOZZLE IT SQUEEZES A SPRING,
WHICH OPENS THE VALVE. THE
INSTANT THIS HAPPENS, SOME OF
THE PRESSURE ON THE PROPELLANT
IS RELEASED, AND THE PROPELLANT
ESCAPES AS A GAS. THE LIQUID THAT
IS INSIDE THE CAN IS CARRIED
ALONG.

You can make your own aerosol bubbling foam bomb. Since it will spray quite far, plan on doing this outdoors or in the bathtub.

HERE IS WHAT YOU NEED:

an empty clear plastic liquid detergent bottle. It should be the kind that has a screw-on, pull-valve cap.

liquid detergent

vinegar

measuring cup

water

VINE

BAKING SODA

I'M READY TO OPERATE!

a funnel with an end that is small enough to fit into the bottle.

measuring spoons

baking soda

FIRST MAKE SURE THAT THE VALVE ON THE DETERGENT BOTTLE CAP IS IN THE CLOSED POSITION. UNSCREW THE TOP. PUT 1/2 CUP (120 MILLILITERS) OF VINEGAR, 1/2 CUP (120 MILLILITERS) OF WATER, AND 1/2 TEASPOON (2.5 MILLILITERS) OF DETERGENT IN THE BOTTLE.

THE NEXT PART IS TRICKY BECAUSE YOU HAVE TO MOVE QUICKLY. PUT THE FUNNEL IN THE MOUTH OF THE BOTTLE. DUMP 1 TABLESPOON (15 MILLILITERS) OF BAKING SODA SO IT SLIDES QUICKLY INTO THE BOTTLE.

Screw on the cap as fast as you can. Shake the bottle. See how it fills with foam. The vinegar and baking soda combine to form carbon dioxide gas, which makes bubbles in the detergent. The bottle will swell under the pressure as the gas forms with no place to go.

Point the cap away from you, into the bathtub or into an open space outside. Don't aim at anyone's face! Pull the valve open. There you have it—a foam explosion of your very own!

45

9 SPURTS, SPOUTS, AND SPRAYS

Many modern inventions squirt liquids. Sometimes the squirting liquid is hidden. Here are some inventions that use spurts, spouts, sprays, hydraulic lifts, valves, and pumps.

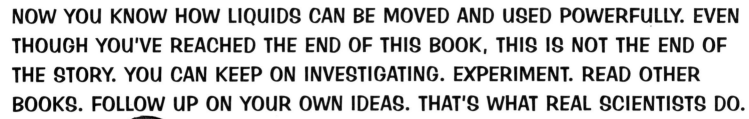

NOW YOU KNOW HOW LIQUIDS CAN BE MOVED AND USED POWERFULLY. EVEN THOUGH YOU'VE REACHED THE END OF THIS BOOK, THIS IS NOT THE END OF THE STORY. YOU CAN KEEP ON INVESTIGATING. EXPERIMENT. READ OTHER BOOKS. FOLLOW UP ON YOUR OWN IDEAS. THAT'S WHAT REAL SCIENTISTS DO.